GLOBAL WARMING

BY JESSICA GUNDERSON

CREATIVE EDUCATION

Published by Creative Education
P.O. Box 227, Mankato, Minnesota 56002
Creative Education is an imprint of
The Creative Company
www.thecreativecompany.us

Design and production by The Design Lab
Art direction by Rita Marshall
Printed by Corporate Graphics in the
United States of America

Photographs by Alamy (ARCTIC IMAGES,
Robert Fried, North Wind Picture Archives),
Dreamstime (Frhojdysz, Hou Guima,
Katemichaela, Leksele, Daniel Leppens,
Martinmark, Photochris, Rodiks, Gina Smith,
Matt Trommer), Getty Images (Cristina
Quicler/AFP), iStockphoto (John Kropewnicki,
Erlend Kvalsvik, Klaas Lingbeek-van Kranen,
Tammy Peluso, Chad Purser, Kirill Putchenko,
Christian Sawicki, Ana Sousa, Stephen
Strathdee, Jan Will)

Library of Congress
Cataloging-in-Publication Data
Gunderson, Jessica.
Global warming / by Jessica Gunderson.
p. cm. — (Earth issues)
Includes bibliographical references and index.
Summary: An examination of the causes and
potential effects of increasing global tempera-
tures, exploring how humans and natural phe-
nomena are involved, as well as how people
can contribute to a healthier planet.
ISBN 978-1-58341-982-3
1. Global warming—Juvenile literature. 2.
Climatic changes—Environmental aspects—
Juvenile literature. I. Title. II. Series.

QC981.8.G56G856 2010
363.738'74—dc22   2009028051

CPSIA: 120109 PO1091
First Edition
9 8 7 6 5 4 3 2 1

Table of Contents

Everything human beings need to survive—air to breathe, food to eat, water to drink—is found on Earth, and on Earth alone. Yet the very planet that sustains human life has come under threat because of human activities. Rivers are drying up as people divert water for their own use. Temperatures are warming as greenhouse gases such as carbon dioxide trap heat in the **atmosphere**. Species of plants and animals are disappearing as people destroy essential habitats. And the rate of many such changes appears to be accelerating. "If I had to use one word to describe the environmental state of the planet right now, I think I would say precarious," said population expert Robert Engelman. "It isn't doomed. It isn't certainly headed toward disaster. But it's in a very precarious situation right now."

One of the biggest threats facing Earth is global warming. The average global temperature is steadily rising, causing polar ice to melt, sea levels to rise, and strong storms to brew. Most scientists believe that the rising temperatures are partially caused by human actions and could bring on mass extinctions and other disasters. As Al Gore, former vice president of the United States and 2007 Nobel Peace Prize winner, warned, "We will face a string of terrible catastrophes unless we act to prepare ourselves and deal with the underlying causes of global warming." But what exactly are the causes? Are humans really at fault? And what can we do to stop global warming before life on Earth is destroyed?

Earth's climate—the long-term weather conditions throughout the world over a period of time—is constantly changing. Over the planet's 4.6 billion years of existence, many natural changes in climate have occurred. For instance, ice ages, or periods in which large portions of the earth have been covered with sheets of ice, have occurred at regular intervals for the past two million years. Between ice ages, warming spells called interglacial periods caused the widespread snow and ice to melt and created the conditions that sustain life on the planet today. Climate scientists called climatologists study such changes and have been keeping detailed records of Earth's climate for the past 150 years. What they have seen in the past three decades has been cause for alarm: Earth's temperature is rapidly increasing and shows no signs of stopping. Although many scientists believe that global warming is natural to an extent, most agree that human activity has quickened its pace.

CHAPTER ONE

An Atmosphere of Life

Life on Earth is sustained in large part thanks to the protective nature of the atmosphere. Stretching from the surface of the earth to about 600 miles (966 km) into space, the atmosphere is held close to the earth due to gravity. It is divided into four successive layers, which, from bottom to top, are the troposphere, stratosphere, mesosphere, and ionosphere, or thermosphere. The atmosphere is made up primarily of a colorless, odorless gas called nitrogen. The remainder (about 22 percent) is mostly oxygen, with small amounts of water vapor, carbon dioxide, and several other gases.

The combination of gases in the troposphere make up what is known as air. Air is essential to life. Humans, animals, and plants

Northern Europe's largest glacier, Norway's Jostedalsbreen, may be protected by a national park but is threatened by a warming planet.

An overabundance of emissions from coal-burning power plants can interfere with the natural processes of the carbon cycle.

use elements found in the air to change food into energy. Two critical elements in this conversion process are oxygen and carbon, and the movement of these elements within and between the air, the earth, and all living things is described by the oxygen and carbon cycles. A process called photosynthesis is critical to both cycles. In photosynthesis, plants absorb sunlight and use that energy to combine carbon gas, or carbon dioxide, with water to produce sugars. In the process, water molecules are split, which releases oxygen into the atmosphere. Animals, on the other hand, breathe in oxygen and exhale carbon dioxide during **respiration**. Thus, the carbon and oxygen cycles work together to maintain a balance of oxygen and carbon in the atmosphere.

The carbon cycle circulates carbon by photosynthesis and respiration, as well as by other means. Plants contain large amounts of carbon, so when they burn or decay, they release carbon dioxide into the air. Over millions of years, dead plants beneath the earth's surface compact and become fossil fuels such as oil, coal, and natural gas. Burning fossil fuels releases carbon dioxide into the atmosphere. Oceans, which absorb vast amounts of carbon dioxide, release some of it back into the air and dissolve the rest into carbonic acid. This cyclical exchange of carbon between land, oceans, and the atmosphere is vital to all plant and animal life.

In droplet form, water vapor helps to form the clouds that cool the earth, release precipitation, and beautify a common sunset.

Warming World

The Union of Concerned Scientists (UCS) is an American nonprofit organization aimed at protecting the environment and making the world a safer place in which to live. The UCS was founded in 1969 and now has more than 250,000 members who are united in their concern for the planet's health. The organization uses both independent research and citizen action to persuade governments to adopt changes and solutions to environmental issues. Global warming is one of the organization's top priorities, and one of its most recent successes was bringing deforestation to the forefront of global warming discussions.

The atmosphere not only contains gases that sustain life, but it also helps keep Earth at a moderate temperature that allows plants and animals to thrive. This is called the greenhouse effect. The greenhouse effect was first proposed in 1827 by French scientist Jean-Baptiste Fourier, who compared Earth's atmosphere to the glass of a greenhouse. The sun's warmth penetrates the glass structure of the greenhouse, warming the air inside. When the sun goes down, the glass traps the heat inside, keeping the air warm even without the sun's rays. Greenhouse gases in the atmosphere operate in a similar way. The gases form a blanket around Earth, keeping the planet's temperature at an average of 57 °F (14 °C). Without the greenhouse effect, Earth's average temperature would be about 0 °F (–17.8 °C), much too cold to sustain life.

The most abundant greenhouse gases are water vapor, carbon dioxide, methane, nitrous oxide, and **ozone**. For thousands of years, the balance between these gases remained the same. However, over the past 150 years, humans have released more and more of these gases into the air. Since the **Industrial Revolution**, humans have increasingly relied upon machines for transportation, heating and cooling, and manufacturing goods. These machines are often powered by the burning of fossil fuels, which releases carbon dioxide into the atmosphere. In 1905, Swedish scientist Svante Arrhenius suggested that the carbon emissions from burning fuels could cause problems for the planet. As humans burned more fossil fuels, Arrhenius warned, the carbon cycle's natural balance would be upset. He predicted that the presence of a higher level of greenhouse gases in the atmosphere could cause the planet to warm.

Carbon dioxide is the most prevalent greenhouse gas emitted by human activities. Since the beginning of the Industrial Revolution, the amount of carbon dioxide in the atmosphere

Although smokestacks were first used during the 1600s, the tall chimneys became widely associated with the later Industrial Revolution.

has increased by an estimated 31 percent. For many years, scientists believed that natural environments known as carbon sinks, such as forests and oceans, would always be able to soak up the excess carbon dioxide. However, in the past few decades, humans have been generating more carbon dioxide than these sinks can absorb. Excess carbon dioxide is then released into the atmosphere, making the greenhouse gases' blanket around Earth thicker and warming the globe in what is known as the enhanced greenhouse effect. Scientists estimate that carbon dioxide accounts for nearly a quarter of all global warming.

In order to fully understand the effects humans have had on the earth, scientists must study the planet's climate history. They can closely estimate Earth's prior climate patterns by using vari-

Most ice core studies are performed in Greenland or Antarctica, and some have revealed climatic data more than 400,000 years old.

Warming World

Water vapor is the most abundant greenhouse gas and the biggest contributor to the natural greenhouse effect. However, because the amount of water in the atmosphere—whether a vapor (gas), liquid, or solid—never changes, it does not contribute to the enhanced greenhouse effect. The concentration of water vapor in the air, known as humidity, can change, however. High levels of humidity increase warming because water vapor, as a greenhouse gas, keeps heat from escaping. But high levels of water vapor can actually help cool the earth, too, by causing clouds to form. Clouds reflect the sun's energy away from the earth, producing a cooling effect.

ous methods of dating certain natural objects such as trees and ice. Scientists study tree rings by slicing open a section of an old tree. Each year, trees grow a new layer of bark, creating a ring around the older layers. During wet years, the ring is thicker, so examining the thickness of the ring helps scientists estimate the precipitation and other climatic factors of that year. Climatologists also study ice cores. Some ice in polar **latitudes** is hundreds to thousands of years old and contains pockets of gas that are trapped within it. Drilling into the ice and studying the gas trapped in these pockets helps scientists determine the makeup of the atmosphere during that time period. Further, the ice core studies have shown a direct **correlation** between higher levels of carbon dioxide in the air and an increased average temperature of the planet.

Using the data obtained by studying Earth's climate history, scientists have been able to determine that in the last 100 years, Earth's average temperature has risen 1 °F (0.6 °C). Although that number may seem insignificant, even a small increase in temperature has a large impact on the planet, causing polar ice caps to melt, sea levels to rise, and droughts, storms, and floods to occur with greater frequency. Scientists warn that average global temperatures may increase by up to 7.2 °F (4.3 °C) by the year 2100, in large part due to the continued release of greenhouse gases into the atmosphere.

Most scientists believe that humans have caused the rapid climate change the earth has been experiencing lately. Human activities, especially burning fuel for energy, have emitted excessive amounts of greenhouse gases into the air; in the 1990s alone, nearly 8 billion tons (7.3 billion t) of carbon dioxide were released each year. Many scientists believe that if the world doesn't change its ways, by the year 2020, people will be emitting 11 billion tons (10 billion t) of carbon dioxide annually.

CHAPTER TWO

Emitting the Problem

Because people in most regions of the world rely on fossil fuels to supply their energy needs, the carbon-rich fuels account for the majority of the harmful emissions. Coal and natural gas are used for electricity and heating, while oil is used for transportation. Cars and trucks run on gasoline, which is a flammable liquid made from **crude oil**. Every day, Americans burn more than 800 million gallons (3.03 billion l) of gasoline. The U.S. uses more than two-fifths of the world's oil supply, and most of it goes toward gasoline. Some **developing countries**, such as China, also use large amounts of fossil fuels. It is estimated that by the year 2030, China will import as much oil as the U.S. does today.

Carbon sinks no longer have the capacity to absorb all of the excess carbon dioxide being released by burning such fuels, and to add to the problem, many such sinks are disappearing. In the oceans, **phytoplankton** absorb large amounts of carbon dioxide for use in photosynthesis. But in recent years, ocean pollution has been killing phytoplankton, and more carbon dioxide therefore goes into the atmosphere.

Deforestation—removing vegetation to make room for buildings, houses, roads, and farmland—reduces the supply of available

Like its relative in the seaweed family, algae, ocean-growing kelp has the potential to be harvested and made into a fuel to rival oil.

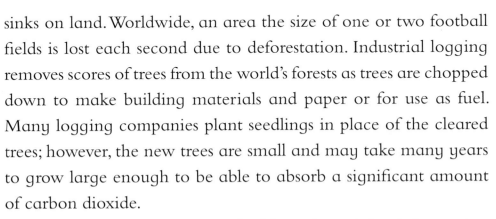

sinks on land. Worldwide, an area the size of one or two football fields is lost each second due to deforestation. Industrial logging removes scores of trees from the world's forests as trees are chopped down to make building materials and paper or for use as fuel. Many logging companies plant seedlings in place of the cleared trees; however, the new trees are small and may take many years to grow large enough to be able to absorb a significant amount of carbon dioxide.

In addition to removing valuable carbon sinks, deforestation also increases atmospheric carbon dioxide directly. In some parts of the world, forests are cleared, and then the land is used for slash-and-burn agriculture. First, trees are chopped down and removed, and the tree stumps that remain are burned. The ash from the burned stumps adds nutrients to the soil, making it good for short-term farming, but the act of burning turns the carbon stored inside the stumps into carbon dioxide, releasing it directly into the atmosphere.

Deforestation in the Amazon makes way for growing soybeans and raising cattle, but it crowds out exotic species of plants and animals.

Warming World

In 1999, an American eighth grader named Claire Lackner conducted a science experiment that used a fish tank and pump to pull carbon dioxide from the air. Her project gave her father, Klaus, a scientist at Columbia University, an idea. He developed a **synthetic** tree that captures carbon dioxide from the air. The trees are approximately 300 feet (91 m) tall and 2 feet (0.6 m) wide and are about 1,000 times more effective than living trees. In a year, one synthetic tree can absorb and store the carbon dioxide emissions equivalent to 7,300 cars. Lackner hopes to have a full-scale model of the synthetic tree available for testing by the year 2012.

Approximately 90 percent of the world's rice fields are located in Asia, and many are terraced to fit the rugged landscape.

Carbon dioxide is not the only greenhouse gas responsible for global warming. Methane, which can also occur naturally, is the second-most abundant greenhouse gas that is increasing due to human activity. Methane traps 20 times more heat than carbon dioxide and is a major concern to climatologists. Landfills are the main culprits of methane emissions because, as waste decomposes, or breaks down, methane is released. Another source of methane comes from grazing livestock such as cows. When cows digest food, they release methane as a byproduct. In one day, a cow can release anywhere from 50 to 150 gallons (189–568 l) of methane. Rice fields also produce methane. Rice is grown on flooded fields, and because the soil is so wet and cannot receive oxygen, the **organic** matter present in the soil breaks down and releases methane. Additionally, when people drill for oil, the drills cut into methane pockets found in the earth, releasing methane into the air.

Nitrous oxide is another greenhouse gas that humans generate. Car exhaust, factory smokestacks, and fertilizers used on farms all produce nitrous oxide. Nitrous oxide levels have increased 18 percent since the beginning of the Industrial Revolution. Human-made chemicals also contribute to the enhanced greenhouse effect. Chemical compounds known as chlorofluorocarbons (CFCs) were developed in the 1930s and were commonly used as coolants in refrigerators, air conditioners, and freezers until the 1970s, when scientists realized the dangers of the gas. CFCs remain in the atmosphere for up to 100 years and trap more heat than any other greenhouse gas.

The world's increasing population is putting a strain on available resources and adding more greenhouse gases to the atmosphere. As the current world population of 6.8 billion increases, more people will need fossil fuels for heating and transportation

Warming World

In the 1970s, scientists discovered that the ozone layer in the upper atmosphere was thinning, and in 1985, an "ozone hole" was found in the stratosphere over Antarctica. People often believe that the ozone hole and global warming are related; however, the ozone hole was not caused by global warming. Instead, the ozone was depleted in large part by human-made CFCs. In the upper atmosphere, ozone intercepts the sun's harmful ultraviolet (UV) rays, protecting humans from skin cancer, eye damage, and other problems. CFCs are now illegal in most countries, and the ozone hole is on the mend.

purposes. More crops for food will need to be grown, and the machines that harvest those crops will emit more greenhouse gases. In addition, more fertilizers will be used to enrich the soil, releasing nitrous oxide into the air and into nearby water supplies as well.

Along with a rising population, the world is witnessing a growing middle class. More middle-class people now own their own cars. They also often live in single-family houses and own products such as stereos, computers, and televisions. Natural resources are needed to manufacture these electronic products, and energy is needed to use them. Energy use emits greenhouse gases, drains the earth of its natural fossil fuels, and creates waste.

The invention of cars, airplanes, and trains has made transportation easier for almost all people. People are able to travel from place to place quickly, and many people commute several miles to get to their workplaces. People also travel to visit friends and family or to go on vacation. The commuter lifestyle has contributed to the emission of greenhouse gases, as car exhaust releases nitrous oxide and carbon gases into the air, and travel by train and airplane uses fossil fuels as well. Some experts say air travel is particularly damaging to the environment because the airplanes emit gases and other pollutants directly into the upper troposphere and lower stratosphere.

Aircraft account for approximately three percent of the planet's total greenhouse gas emissions, which could grow if not checked.

Some debate lingers over whether high levels of greenhouse gases directly cause global warming, but the evidence is clear that warming is occurring. Areas near the poles are warming faster than the rest of the globe. Over the past 50 years, temperatures have risen about 5.4 °F (3 °C) in the Arctic and 4.5 °F (2.5 °C) in the Antarctic. These warmer temperatures have caused age-old snow and ice to melt. For instance, the Larsen B Ice Shelf, a 12,000-year-old area of Antarctic ice, broke up in a matter of months in 2002. But large-scale melting is not restricted to polar regions; Montana's Glacier National Park contained 150 glaciers in 1910, but today, only 37 of those glaciers still exist. The U.S. government estimates that there will be no glaciers remaining in the national park by the year 2030.

CHAPTER THREE

Warming Effects

The melting ice caps, snow, and glaciers heighten the effects of global warming. Because ice and snow are white, they reflect about 90 percent of the light from the sun. The percentage of reflected sunlight is called albedo. When an area warms and the snow or ice melts, it exposes darker land or sea. Darker colors are less reflective and absorb more heat, causing Earth's temperature to rise. The higher temperatures cause more ice and snow to melt, and the cycle continues in what is called the albedo effect.

Melting snow and ice also affect sea levels. As the snow and ice on land melt, water runs into lakes and rivers, which flow into the oceans, and the ice already present in oceans melts directly into the water. Even without the melting sea ice, though, sea levels are rising because of higher global temperatures that have caused entire bodies of water to warm and expand. Higher sea levels can endanger coastal communities around the world. Seaside cities

Montana's towering Mission Mountains are close to Glacier National Park and also contain glaciers and year-round snowfields.

The Netherlands, with its many islands and peninsulas, constructed a series of dams and moveable barriers called the Delta Works between 1950 and 1997.

such as New Orleans, Louisiana; Rio de Janeiro, Brazil; and Shanghai, China, would face certain flooding, and low-lying countries such as the Netherlands, Bangladesh, and the island nation of the Maldives are concerned about losing their inhabitants, **economic** independence, and entire way of life. The Netherlands has built **dikes** and drainage systems to combat the rising waters, but other countries in similar straits do not have the physical or financial resources to undertake such projects.

Meanwhile, freshwater supplies are being hurt by rising sea levels. When salt water from the oceans spills over into freshwater lakes and rivers, fresh water used for drinking and **irrigation** becomes contaminated. The proportion of fresh water available to the amount withdrawn is called water stress. High water stress indicates that there is a small ratio of supply to the amount needed. By the year 2025, experts estimate that 60 percent of the world's population will live in areas of mid to high water stress.

Known as "the rainforests of the oceans," coral reefs form in shallow, clear water, which gives the algae access to light.

Warming World

Coral reefs are complex underwater structures built from the hard outer skeletons of individual animals called coral polyps. Found in tropical waters, coral reefs are important to marine life; one in four sea creatures spends at least part of its life among coral reefs. Coral reefs also provide natural barriers that protect many tropical coastlines from the full force of the ocean's waves. However, the reefs are suffering damage from climate change, mostly due to coral bleaching. Corals get their color and food from algae that grow near them, but warmer ocean temperatures have caused algae to disappear. The corals then "bleach," or turn white and die.

From space, a hurricane's power is clearly visible, and weather satellites that orbit Earth can warn people of impending storms.

The coastal city of New Orleans, Louisiana, experienced the full fury of Hurricane Katrina, with widespread flooding and damage.

The warming oceans contribute to changing weather patterns. As the ocean's surface warms, water evaporates, which increases the energy in the atmosphere. The heightened energy in the atmosphere can produce more instances of extreme weather, such as hurricanes and tornadoes. In 2005, the earth experienced the most catastrophic storms on record. In August of that year, Hurricane Katrina ravaged the coast along the Gulf of Mexico, killing more than 1,300 people and displacing millions. Homes, businesses, factories, and roads were destroyed by the hurricane. Although global warming is not the only cause of such extreme weather, many climatologists agree that the overall warming temperatures contribute to such storms.

Some areas of the globe have recently experienced heat waves that lasted for days or even months. Many areas are unused to such high temperatures, and people often do not have the resources, such as air conditioning, necessary to combat the heat. In 2003, a heat wave in Europe caused at least 30,000 deaths.

Rising global temperatures also contribute to desertification, or the process by which land is turned into desert. High heat combined with low levels of precipitation can cause desertification, as can droughts, which are also becoming increasingly more common. A drought is a period with little to no precipitation. Droughts can destroy food crops and water supplies. In less-wealthy countries that depend heavily upon agriculture, failed crops can mean widespread starvation. These countries may not have the funds to feed their people if the food supply is low.

Climate change affects plant and animal species around the world, most notably the polar bear. Polar bears travel across permanent sea ice and use floating ice to hunt for seals, but because of rapid melting, their hunting options are shrinking. In addition, the ice that forms every winter is melting sooner than usual, sometimes stranding the bears, which are then unable to **migrate** to summer hunting grounds. Extended periods without food have caused their populations to dwindle, and in 2007, the U.S. Geological Survey warned that if polar ice continues to melt, two-thirds of all polar bears could disappear by 2050.

Although polar bears are classified as "threatened," some activists want them further protected by the U.S. Endangered Species Act.

Warming World

The golden toad was the first known species to disappear due to global warming. The brilliantly colored toad once lived exclusively in Costa Rica's Monteverde Cloud Forest Reserve. Cloud forests are characterized by an almost constant cloud cover or fog that hovers above the trees, and the golden toad needed these conditions to breed. However, warming of the surrounding ocean caused the fog to form farther up the mountain, robbing the toad of its habitat and making it more susceptible to disease and direct heat from the sun. First identified in 1966, no one has seen a golden toad since 1989, and the species is considered extinct.

Costa Rica's golden toad, along with other frogs, reptiles, and birds, were all affected by changing climates in the cloud forest.

In other areas, as the temperatures increase, cold-weather species are moving away to find cooler habitats, living closer to the poles or climbing to higher **altitudes**. Birds' migratory patterns are changing, with some birds ceasing to migrate at all due to increasingly milder winters. Species that are unable to adapt to the changing climate are at risk of becoming extinct, and extinct species can upset the natural balance of a habitat's **food chain**.

Human health, too, is affected by climate changes when diseases such as **malaria** spread to areas in which they previously did not exist. Malaria is spread by infected mosquitoes and is found mostly in tropical regions surrounding the equator. However, as temperatures warm throughout the globe, infected mosquitoes are spreading to nontropical areas. Higher temperatures also affect the quality of the air people breathe, especially in crowded cities, as warmer air causes smog (a mixture of fog, smoke, and other air pollutants) to linger. High levels of smog can bring on chest pains and asthma attacks.

Habitat loss is a serious threat to many species and the primary cause
of whooping cranes' endangered status in North America.

Because the problems associated with global warming are far-reaching and international in scope, the issue of how to reduce emissions has become a political one for many governments. Some politicians argue that it would cost too much money to change from fossil fuels to other energy sources. Others want more proof about the detrimental effects of global warming; they say that there is not a **consensus** among scientists. However, in 2007, the International Panel on Climate Change (IPCC) concluded that the warming that has occurred over the last 50 years cannot be explained without taking human activity into account. Most prominent scientists and major scientific organizations have accepted the IPCC's statement as accurate, and more politicians are conceding that climate change is a reality that the world must face.

CHAPTER FOUR

A Worldwide Effort

The human effect on the environment has been recognized as cause for worldwide concern since the 1970s. At the first World Climate Conference in 1979, many scientists warned that human activity could cause climate change, and countries realized then that reducing greenhouse gas emissions would have to be a global effort in order to make a difference. Since 1992, 192 nations have signed the United Nations Framework Convention on Climate Change (UNFCCC), an international treaty that binds nations to work together to combat global warming.

In 1997, delegates from 170 nations met in Kyoto, Japan, to discuss the climate change problem and signed an addition to the UNFCCC called the Kyoto Protocol. According to the Kyoto Protocol, by the year 2012, industrialized countries would reduce greenhouse gas emissions by an average of 5.2 percent below

Al Gore spearheads a global training program called The Climate Project, whose volunteers educate the public on climate issues.

Warming World

Former U.S. vice president Al Gore is an influential **advocate** of the movement to reduce global warming. He first became interested in environmental studies as a college student at Harvard. He remained involved in environmental issues throughout his life and career in politics, publishing his first book, *Earth in the Balance*, in 1992. His documentary film and companion book, *An Inconvenient Truth*, directly address the consequences of and solutions to global warming. The documentary won an Academy Award in 2007 and is considered one of the most influential documentaries of the 21st century. For his work on environmental issues, Gore received the 2007 Nobel Peace Prize.

1990 levels. Countries still in development, such as China, India, and many African nations, would not have to meet the same targets because doing so could hinder the developing nations' growth. The U.S., the world's top greenhouse gas producer, supported the Kyoto Protocol in 1997 but never **ratified** it, explaining in 2001 that adhering to such tight restrictions would hurt the U.S. economy and that the terms were unfair because developing countries did not have to follow the same rules.

Many nations were discouraged by the U.S.'s rejection of the Kyoto Protocol, but the efforts to stop global warming did not end there. Delegates from more than 190 countries, including the U.S., continue to meet under the UNFCCC to propose international strategies for dealing with greenhouse gas emissions. As the Kyoto Protocol is set to expire in 2012, members of the UNFCCC are gearing up to negotiate terms for a new global warming treaty.

Although China is classed as a developing country, it has a booming industrial sector that emits dangerous amounts of pollutants.

Offshore wind turbines are possible in Denmark, thanks to expanses of relatively shallow water that surround the country.

Although international agreements represent a significant step toward slowing global warming, scientists say it is not enough. In order to stabilize atmospheric levels of greenhouse gases by the middle of the 21st century, we must reduce emissions to 60 percent below 2005 levels. The greatest challenge in reducing emissions is to cut our dependency on fossil fuels by using clean, renewable energy sources. Wind, solar, and hydro (water) power are sources of clean energy—energy that does not emit greenhouse gases or waste. Many countries such as Germany, Spain, and Denmark are already using wind energy as a major source of power; even in the U.S., giant wind turbines have been placed in exceptionally windy areas such as the Great Plains. Wind spins the blades on the turbines, which are connected to generators that create electricity.

The hydroelectricity plant at the foot of the Glen Canyon Dam on the Colorado River provides power to some 5.8 million customers.

Hydropower works in much the same way. Ocean waves and waterfalls hold large amounts of energy. Waterwheels can be placed in areas with water movement. The movement of water spins the wheels and generates electricity. Another powerful source of clean energy is the sun. The sun's energy is captured in solar panels that are placed on homes, power plants, and other buildings. Inside the panels are solar cells containing thin layers

Warming World

One of the main reasons people use fossil fuels is because they are cheap forms of energy. Environmentalists worry that most nations and factories will choose the cheaper energy sources rather than investing in more Earth-friendly alternatives. They argue that, at the very least, we need to make fossil fuels cleaner, and one way to do this is by using clean coal technology at coal-fired power plants. Clean coal technology captures carbon dioxide before it is released into the air, then pumps it underground for storage. Implementing clean coal technology is expensive, however, and experts say it is decades away from being perfected for widespread use.

of **silicon**. When sunlight hits the cell, the silicon absorbs the sun's energy, and electrical charges move between the silicon layers to produce an electric current.

Another alternative to fossil fuels is **nuclear** energy, since nuclear power plants do not release greenhouse gases. France receives almost three-fourths of its energy from nuclear power. However, the development of nuclear power plants is a controversial issue for many reasons, not the least of which is that the process is potentially dangerous to humans and the environment. To produce energy, atoms of the metal uranium are split in a process called nuclear fission. When the atom is split, small particles called neutrons are released and bump against other atoms, splitting them and resulting in a chain reaction of nuclear fission. If the chain reaction is not tightly controlled, explosions can occur. Fission releases heat that is used to boil water, which then spins turbines to generate electricity. But **radiation** is also released during fission, and if humans are exposed to high levels of radiation, they can develop cancer and other illnesses.

Moving away from our dependence on fossil fuels is a long process that may take many years. Governments are realizing they need to offer financial **incentives** or penalties in order to speed up the necessary changes. Some have considered issuing a carbon tax, which would charge a fee to companies and factories that use fossil fuels. Another viable option is carbon trading, in which a cap is placed on emissions, and companies hold a set number of emission allowances, or credits, which cannot exceed the cap. Companies whose emissions go beyond the cap must buy credits from companies with emissions lower than the cap. Therefore, companies with lower emissions can benefit financially.

Transportation uses much of the world's oil supply. As the stock of oil continues to be depleted, and as Earth heats up, automakers are designing more fuel-efficient cars or cars that

Nuclear power plants are easily recognizable by the concrete cooling towers that dominate the surrounding lonely landscape.

All biogas plants follow a similar general pattern of construction, beginning with a circular pit design and a vertical metal pipe.

Warming World

Biogas is an alternative source of energy that is produced from the decomposition of organic material—matter that has come from a once-living organism—in the absence of oxygen. Rotting plants, garbage dumps, and animal waste all produce methane, which, when mixed with oxygen, is combustible. Gobar gas is a type of biogas made from cow dung. At the Gobar Gas Research Station in Ajitmal, India, researchers have designed many gobar gas plants for use around the country. At the gas plants, cow manure is thrown into airtight, circular pits. The manure produces methane gas, which is then piped out for use in people's homes.

run on biofuels, such as ethanol. Biofuels are derived from plants and are considered a renewable energy source. Vehicles powered solely by biofuels do not emit carbon dioxide. Another popular alternative is the hybrid car. Hybrids combine a fuel-powered motor with an electric one. The electric motor powers the car at low speeds, and the action of the brakes recharges the motor. While hybrids do use gasoline, they don't need to use nearly as much as traditional cars.

As researchers and governments develop ways to combat global warming, individuals can also play a part in the fight for the earth's life. Turning off lights, appliances, televisions, and computers when they are not in use can help reduce electricity and the greenhouse gases emitted due to its production. Making fewer trips in the car and taking public transportation whenever possible can unclog roadways and decrease air pollution due to carbon emissions. Once people realize that making even small changes in their lifestyles may help save the entire planet, the threats of global warming will be minimized, and the earth will stand a better chance of remaining a thriving, livable planet fit for many future generations.

Canola oil comes from the yellow-flowered rape plant and, though commonly used for cooking, may soon become a viable biofuel.

Warming World

A good way to help curb global warming is to reduce your "carbon footprint." A carbon footprint is the amount of greenhouse gases produced by burning fossil fuels to support your lifestyle. You can reduce your carbon footprint by making simple changes around your home. Exchanging a standard shower head for a low-flow model will reduce the amount of energy used to heat the water. Replacing all regular light bulbs with compact fluorescents will use about four-fifths less energy and save on electricity costs. Drying clothes on a clothesline is also better for the environment, and it will help reduce your footprint, too.

Hanging even one load of laundry outside to dry can prevent the emission of more than five pounds (2.3 kg) of carbon dioxide.

Glossary

advocate—a person who publicly supports and recommends an idea or plan

altitudes—heights of objects in relation to sea level

atmosphere—the layer of gases that surrounds Earth

consensus—a general agreement among all involved

correlation—a mutual relationship or connection between two or more things

crude oil—oil in its natural state, before it is made into gasoline

developing countries—the poorest countries of the world, which are generally characterized by a lack of health care, nutrition, education, and industry; most developing countries are in Africa, Asia, and Latin America

dikes—long, high walls built to hold back water and prevent flooding

economic—relating to the economy, the social system that involves production and consumption of a country's wealth, goods, and services

food chain—a system in nature in which living things are dependent on each other for food

incentives—things, such as money, that motivate people to take specific actions

Industrial Revolution—a period during the late 18th and early 19th centuries in Europe and the U.S., marked by a shift from economies based on agriculture and handicraft to ones dominated by mechanized production in factories

irrigation—the distribution of water to land or crops to help plant growth

latitudes—regions referenced by their temperature and distance north or south from the equator

malaria—a sometimes fatal disease caused by parasites that is spread by mosquitoes to animals and people

migrate—to move from one region or habitat to another, especially when the seasons change

nuclear—having to do with energy created when atoms are split or joined together

organic—derived from or relating to living matter

ozone—a toxic gas made up of three oxygen atoms; in the stratosphere, the ozone layer contains a high concentration of ozone, which helps to protect Earth from the sun's harmful rays

phytoplankton—microscopic plants that drift along near the surface of large bodies of water

radiation—the emission of radioactive materials, which release energy in the form of heat and light

ratified—formally approved a treaty or agreement so that it could take effect

respiration—the process by which animals take in oxygen and release carbon dioxide

silicon—a chemical element found in sand and rocks, often used in making electronics, glass, and cement

synthetic—made artificially through chemical processes, especially to imitate a natural product

Bibliography

DiMento, Joseph, and Pamela Doughman, eds. *Climate Change: What It Means for Us, Our Children, and Our Grandchildren.* Cambridge, Mass.: Massachusetts Institute of Technology Press, 2007.

Flannery, Tim. *The Weather Makers: How Man Is Changing the Climate and What It Means for Life on Earth.* New York: Atlantic Monthly Press, 2005.

Houghton, John. *Global Warming: The Complete Briefing.* 3rd edition. New York: Cambridge University Press, 2004.

Krupp, Fred, and Miriam Horn. *Earth: The Sequel: The Race to Reinvent Energy and Stop Global Warming.* New York: W. W. Norton, 2008.

Lomborg, Bjorn. *Cool It: The Skeptical Environmentalist's Guide to Global Warming.* New York: Alfred A. Knopf, 2007.

Romm, Joseph J. *Hell and High Water: Global Warming—The Solution and the Politics—and What We Should Do.* New York: HarperCollins, 2007.

U.S. Environmental Protection Agency. "Climate Change." http://www.epa.gov/climatechange/index.html.

Weart, Spencer R. *The Discovery of Global Warming.* Cambridge, Mass.: Harvard University Press, 2003.

For Further Information

Books

Anderson, Dale. *Al Gore: A Wake-up Call to Global Warming*.
New York: Crabtree Publishing, 2009.

Oxlade, Chris. *Global Warming*. Mankato, Minn.: Capstone Press, 2003.

Silverstein, Alvin, Virginia Silverstein, and Laura Silverstein Nunn. *Global
Warming*. Brookfield, Conn.: Twenty-First Century Books, 2003.

Unwin, Mike. *Planet Under Pressure: Climate Change*. Chicago: Heinemann Library, 2007.

Web Sites

EPA Climate Change Kids Site
http://epa.gov/climatechange/kids/index.html

The Pew Center on Global Warming: Global Warming—Kids Page
http://www.pewclimate.org/global-warming-basics/kidspage.cfm

National Geographic: Global Warming Facts, Causes, Effects, Solutions
http://environment.nationalgeographic.com/environment/global-warming/

ThinkQuest: Global Warming
http://library.thinkquest.org/CR0215471/global_warming.htm

Index